Personal Organization for Degenerates

Brandon Adams

Copyright © 2017 Brandon Adams

All rights reserved.

ISBN: 1521498202
ISBN-13: 9781521498200

CONTENTS

1	Managed Dissolution	1
2	Health	4
3	Money	13
4	Time	20
5	Competitive Edge and Career Planning	27
6	Tilt, or Sensitive Dependence on Initial Conditions	31

1 MANAGED DISSOLUTION

At my brother's rehearsal dinner, I noted that he was a "jolly degenerate," and it didn't go over super-well. For me, degenerate is a term of endearment.

A degenerate person, in casting the present against the future, makes decisions that appear unwise and inconsistent. Degenerates are wired in such a way that they strongly value the present over the future. This is a book about how people with degenerate wiring can nonetheless manage their affairs intelligently.

Having read many books on personal organization, I've been struck by the fact that there are no books aimed at people who are, at their core, degenerates. As a reasonably organized degenerate, I've taken it upon myself to fill this gap. Degenerates, you have been underserved. No longer.

Most books about personal organization are written by highly capable people trying to become more capable. The underlying assumption of most personal organization books is that time freed up by personal organization implies that there will be more time for greater accomplishment. In this way of thinking, productivity and continuous improvement are ends in themselves.

The underlying assumption of *Personal Organization for Degenerates* is that time freed up by personal organization creates more time for unstructured, centrifugal activity, which is inherently more enjoyable. Dissolution is the natural state of life. Time spent on organization is necessary, but real joy comes from the unstructured time that is afforded by the investment you make in getting organized.

My non-degenerate traits that allow me to claim that I am somewhat organized are as follows: taught at Harvard for nine years, graduated college at nineteen, ranked top ten in the country in tennis (men's 30 and over, 2015), have written three books, have two healthy and happy kids (no wife, though), accomplished in poker and sports analytics. My degenerate bona fides are harder to enumerate. I've been one of the biggest gamblers of my generation for fifteen years, and I'm friends or acquaintances with almost everyone else who fits in that category. Though I don't do drugs other than an occasional Adderall, I drink both coffee and wine in huge quantities.

The definition of degenerate, according to the *Oxford Dictionary*, is "having lost the physical, mental, or moral qualities considered normal or desirable; showing evidence of decline." This definition, it seems to me, applies to most people! In fact, one could argue that many real problems come from denying that you are a degenerate. We are all in decline. A life well lived is a life of managed decline.

Now, that said, I have noticed that there are people who possess certain characteristics that make them slightly more degenerate than the general population. These people might benefit especially from this book. Degenerates often have low, or at least highly varying, native energy levels. They tend to be stimulation-oriented, preferring the exploration of new areas to the disciplined pursuit of known opportunities. They crave excitement, and use adrenaline as a key energy source. And, they have, often to their detriment, a tendency to value the short-term over the long-term to an excessive degree. They also tend, from what I gather, to be male.

If you're a non-degenerate, you should nonetheless consider continuing to read this book. Among the positive traits of degenerates are a certain flexibility of thought and a tendency to consider out-of-the-box solutions. I would imagine that some of the organizational solutions I've come up with have merit even for non-degenerates.

This short book is organized simply. The next three chapters will focus on managing your health, managing your money, and managing your time. Chapter Five focuses on career strategy. The final chapter, "Tilt, or Sensitive Dependence on Initial Conditions," focuses on emotional control, or managing your affairs when things aren't going well.

2 HEALTH

This is a chapter on health unlike chapters on health in other books. Said chapters assume that time, energy, and discipline are in almost unlimited supply, whereas this one assumes that you are a degenerate.

If you have kids, your health and their well-being are of equal importance. If you don't, health is your overwhelming consideration. Attention paid to your health is the best investment of time, energy, and money that you can make. Everything else is of secondary importance. I'm 6' 3", 200 pounds, 13 percent body fat. In early 2007, I was the same height and weight, with a bit more body fat. Then, from late April 2007 through August 2007, I lived at the Venetian in Las Vegas, won more money than I thought possible playing poker, and went up to 216 pounds and 24 percent body fat. This was a case of sacrificing health for other factors (money, mostly), and it's almost never worth it. The problem is that health is ruled by vicious cycles, and while human psychology compels us to think that bad choices can be overcome by later good deeds, this is rarely true. The best predictor of current weight for most people is the highest weight they've ever been in their life. Like Peter Gibbons in *Office Space*, for whom "every single day that you see me, that's on the worst day of my life," most people you see on the street are having something close to the fattest day they've ever had in their life.

In matters of health, the importance of virtuous cycles (always somewhat scarce in life) pales in comparison to the importance of vicious cycles. The most important vicious cycles to be aware of are: a breakdown of the body's ability to process carbohydrates that results from consuming them in excess; the conditioning that occurs when your body is exposed to potentially harmful substances, including alcohol, caffeine, or drugs; and the degrading of ability that comes with stress, and the tendency of this degrading of ability to beget yet more stress.

The first vicious cycle relates to perhaps the clearest health mistake you can make: consuming too much sugar and too many carbohydrates. Your body produces insulin to break down sugar in the bloodstream. When the body is asked to do this too often or to too great an extent, it can't do the job properly.

I don't advocate extreme solutions to this problem. My experience is that extremely low-carbohydrate diets are unpleasant. My suggestion for dealing with the sugar and carb problem is this: Cut pure sugars and fruit juices almost completely from your diet, consume simple carbohydrates sparingly, and keep your consumption of all types of carbs to a minimum at night. If you're in weight-cutting mode, stay mostly off carbs, but know that your energy levels will suffer as a result. My advice to avoid sugar almost entirely is one of the more extreme pieces of advice you'll find in this book, but it's one area where the cost-benefit equations and error asymmetries are perfectly clear. Consuming a lot of sugars and simple carbs yields almost no benefits to your body, and there is a potentially catastrophic downside.

The second vicious cycle we should be aware of is the conditioning your body undergoes when potentially harmful substances are ingested. My suggestion here is that, for anything that involves conditioning, you need to have rules of some kind. Now, you will probably break these rules, but you should nonetheless strive to have rules in place.

There's a good case for simply never consuming a potentially addictive substance even one time. I have never tried cocaine, nicotine, and many other drugs, simply because I know I'd probably like them, and so I'm strategically avoiding the possible addictions. Having tried and loved alcohol and caffeine, I'll never quit either and so simply need rules for managing their use. If you find with experience that you're the type of person who can't even keep within the ballpark of the rules you've set for yourself for substances like alcohol, you have to consider quitting altogether.

The third vicious cycle is the stress response. Our nervous system is not like a muscle, where forcing it to deal with stress makes it stronger over time. In most contexts, the opposite is usually true. Stress is the demon of the modern era. It is directly damaging to our health in all kinds of ways. And the more stress we have, the less resilient we become, and the less capable of dealing with further stress. The march of technology is relentless, and nothing about technological advance, from what I've seen, decreases stress on the nervous system. So we would all be wise to carve out as many avenues of stress release for ourselves as we can reasonably afford.

In sports analytics, frequent reference is made to an athlete's "age curve." Physically demanding sports typically see athletes improving their performance up to the mid-twenties; performance then steadily drops off in the thirties before falling off a cliff in the late thirties. When it comes to our own personal age curves—how our abilities change and/or falter with age—we are on our own. Even books dedicated to the subject, such as Robert Bribiescas's *How Men Age*, offer precious few details on what exactly the aging male can expect. And, needless to say, the age curve of the degenerate would seem to be slightly more harsh.

I'm thirty-eight, and no doubt my views on how to optimally navigate aging will change a hundred times in the next couple of decades, but I will share some of my current viewpoints. No one likes losing things, or having change toward the negative, but this is almost the definition of aging when it comes to physical ability. A mental anchoring takes place when we're younger that prevents us from making intelligent adjustments with age. To give yet one example, most middle-aged men still cling to the mental image of hard workouts and intense jogs, and so don't allow themselves to view a calm walk as exercise, but a case could be made that this is the best exercise option available to them.

I have no view yet on hormone therapy, such as testosterone

supplementation or HGH.

If you are otherwise aging well, it's probably wise to avoid these things. Conservatism is generally wise in health decisions because of the asymmetry of the costs and benefits involved. For example, testosterone supplementation might have benefits such as fat loss, improved appearance and strength, and greater energy, but you might be trading these benefits off against possible costs, such as prostate cancer, which are orders of magnitude more risky. That said, aging itself is a beast and not all that conservative, so if your health profile is troubled (say you're sixty and fat and have no energy), then the cost-benefit picture changes drastically, and conservatism in health decisions might be self-defeating. If you're sixty and fat and don't have the energy and motivation to exercise, then you're a strong favorite to die of heart disease, cancer, or stroke in the next ten years, and so if there's a chance that hormone supplementation could spur you toward exercise and fat reduction, it is worth a try.

For degenerates, the administrative effort involved in booking and keeping appointments and tracking health files is a tall order. The ideal modern patient would have all health files on a USB and/or in a Dropbox. For degenerates who can afford it, my recommendation is that you attend an executive health program at least once, and perhaps as often as every two years. The Mayo Executive Health Program (maybe the most efficient operation of any type I've seen) will take any headaches out of scheduling, and will absolutely minimize the frictions associated with going from one appointment to the next. The end result will be a comprehensive, personalized health file that you can move to another doctor or carry around in paper and electronic form.

As you age, managing weight fluctuation becomes increasingly difficult. Only one aspect of this is easy to see and measure: People get fat, and their weight goes up when they're consuming excess calories. There's a subtle aspect that's difficult to see and is underappreciated: Many adults go through cycles where they keep their weight relatively constant but see their muscle mass decrease substantially. Some of this is related to hormone changes and slight decreases in the ability of the body to break down sugar, but these factors might not be primary. What happens to many people is that they gain weight by, for instance, overindulging in short periods of time—say, on a vacation, or in a busy month full of work dinners. The pattern is that weight is added, but almost all of this new weight is fat. Suppose that, after this month of work dinners and limited workouts, you have managed to gain a full ten pounds. A typical response would be to go on a diet to cut the weight. But even if you are successful and manage the weight-loss process well, the absolute best you might do is lose six pounds of fat and four pounds of muscle.

This cycle—gaining mostly fat, then losing a combo of fat and muscle—is the norm. One consequence is that most people will experience an increase in their body fat percentage even if their weight remains stable. Fighting this typical pattern of aging requires a huge amount of work. A good starting point is to strive to keep your weight as stable as possible, and to think of binges as being especially costly.

The simple "calories in, calories out" equation is fundamental to health, but most people have absolutely no idea how many calories they burn in a typical day. This is a huge mistake. You should invest time and money in learning exactly how many calories your body burns at rest and during exercise. There's no shortcut to doing this. You have to go to a gym, get connected to some equipment, and undergo time-consuming, painful, and somewhat expensive tests.

The first is a test of your resting metabolic rate. This will tell you how many calories you burn in a normal day with no activity. For me, it's 2,850 calories, a very high level. This test will require that you lie on a table for 45 minutes with a bubble around your head that captures and measures all carbon dioxide output from your body.

The second one—and it's painful—is a VO2 max test. It's similar to a stress test, but slightly more involved, and it will tell you exactly how many calories your body burns for each level of activity. With the results of a good VO2 max, and a heart rate monitor, you will know, with a fair degree of precision, how many calories your body burns for any type of workout.

For example, my VO2 max stats look like this:

	Baseline	Anaerobic Threshold	Maximum Measured
VO2 (ml O2 / kg / min.)	7	29.4	58.9
Heart Rate (bpm)	71	116	181
Calories per Hour	196	813	1722

Heart Rate	Kcal/Hr
77	233
83	366
91	485
103	607
108	676
118	836
134	1001
149	1235
158	1341
166	1494
174	1621
180	1671

Suppose I wear a heart rate monitor for a one-hour tennis lesson and find that my average heart rate for the session was 134. My total calories burned during that session would be 1,001. The variability of your heart rate around that average of 134 matters, but not much. Your VO2 results and a heart rate monitor will give you an accurate assessment of your calorie burn per workout. You will quickly learn that most estimates of calorie burn to be found on Internet sites and standard-issue gym monitors are worthless. How could it be otherwise, given that they don't take your particular physiology into account?

If I'm trying to cut weight, I find that there is only one thing that works for me, and that is keeping a log of calories in and calories out, and trying to reach some target goal for a cumulative calorie deficit. For example, if I'm trying to lose five pounds, the necessary deficit would be 17,500 calories (3,500 calories per pound × 5 pounds), and I would keep a log of calories in and calories burned until I hit a total deficit of 17,500. Each day starts with my resting metabolic rate of 2,850 calories per day. I add to this burn any activity that I do. I don't track it exactly with a heart rate monitor, but, since I've done this before, I'm pretty good at estimating how many calories my body burns for each level of activity. On the "calories in" side, I find that rough approximations generally suffice. Many restaurant menus have reliable calorie counts; between this and quick Google searches, it's easy to add up how many calories you consume per day.

When you're cutting weight, at some point the costs of doing so will become apparent. Your energy will sag, you will be hungry, you will be irritable. You will reach your personal best steady-state weight by arriving at a balance between the costs and benefits of losing weight. For me, that occurs somewhere around 200 pounds. This is not particularly lean for me. But any bad health decisions you make in your life increase your steady-state best weight. And the decisions I've made over time—bad but not too bad—have resulted in the fact that my body is not especially efficient at converting food to energy, and can't get to low levels of body fat without incurring very high cost.

Although every health decision has consequences that are difficult to quantify, you should nonetheless spend a lot of time thinking about the expected costs and benefits of different health decisions. Again, decisions about health are the most important you'll make. Be cautious in the face of severe asymmetries. If something will be either a little bit good for you or very bad for you, avoid doing it.

Most people are not, broadly speaking, careful enough in matters of personal safety. I have completely unreasonable and unbalanced behavior in many contexts, but as a pedestrian I'll almost always take a long time before crossing a street. In general, if there's some chance that something very, very bad can happen, healthwise, then be cautious. This goes for relatively mundane activities: driving on fast, crowded interstates; experimenting with drugs; taking part in high-risk sports like skiing and snowboarding. When you're driving, proceed as if your life is always in danger. In particular, never take any risks involving a side-impact collision. No matter how many people are honking wildly behind you, if you can't see well enough to assess a traffic situation in full, simply don't move. With regard to decisions about safety, never look to other people for guidance, because terrible decisions are the norm.

There are risks that are continuous in nature. Many things I do are somewhat bad for me, and the more I do them, the worse they are for me. Drinking alcohol is bad, and drinking more alcohol is worse; the same is true of eating heavy meals late at night, eating sugars, eating fried foods, or eating fish known to have some pollutants (this includes most types). These are health risks, but they are manageable risks.

Other types of risks are discontinuous in nature. They are mostly safe until they are not at all safe. Examples of this include psychotropic drug use, risky sexual activity, and anything that involves heavy things moving fast (including driving, biking, fighting, and risky sports). Extreme care should be exercised around anything health-related that has a discontinuous risk profile.

There's a further distinction to be drawn, though, regarding discontinuous risk functions. Some activities, like bike-racing or skiing tree runs, have a discontinuous risk profile (where there is a small probability that, suddenly, something very bad will happen to you). You are taking on this risk profile by simply making a decision to participate. You can manage the risk profile somewhat—by, for instance, taking a cautious route down the mogul run—but the decision to potentially incur risk was made at the beginning, the moment you started down the mountain. A different type of asymmetric risk function involves activities that are only a little bit dangerous until some critical threshold is passed, at which point they become unbelievably dangerous. This is a common profile of drug use, and it is a good reason for caution in that area.

3 MONEY

As a degenerate, you crave novelty. Your relationship with money may be troubled, because you are likely to seek adventures in the form of gambling, trading, or business risk. And as someone who strongly values the present against the future, you're likely to spend quite high in the pursuit of new experiences.

In personal finance and investment, flashiness does not pay, for the most part. Flashy decisions garner all the attention, but the money accrues to the Golden Glove centerfielders of the business world, those who go about their business with maximum efficiency, making a minimum of mistakes. In this chapter, I'm going to go over eight simple rules for degenerate money management.

The "100 Small Bet" Rule

As a degenerate, you love to go "all in," whether with an investment, an idea, a new business, or a romantic partner. This has probably never been a great idea, but it's a particularly terrible idea in 2017. Technology kills the middleman. It kills middle-sized enterprises of every type. We live in an era of promise, because technology allows successful ideas to spread further and faster than ever before. But we also live in an era of great failure. Almost every new idea and business fails. The consequence for individuals is simple: You have to try to succeed many more times than before, and you have to strategize such that the consequences of failure are minimized.

I like to conceptualize this strategy as "100 Small Bets." When you take on a new task and devote all of your time and energy to it, and almost cannot imagine how devastating it would be to fail, you nonetheless have to realize that failure is likely. Over the long term, you might have to take on a hundred projects with similar demands if you expect to be successful.

Recognize the Power of Exponential Growth

Growth in the current period is a function of growth in the previous period. Audience growth is exponential, and many of the world's most powerful businesses experienced rapid exponential audience growth in their infancy. Technology allows new ideas to spread faster than ever before. And because the developed world is wired, exponential growth can proceed for a long time before ever starting to level off.

If you find investments that might benefit from exponential growth, the worst that can happen is that they fail and you lose your initial investments. The best that can happen is that they succeed and you make 10 times or 100 times your investment—or, in the case of a Google or Facebook, a nearly infinite multiple of your initial investment.

The 100 Small Bets rule thus applies to investments of your money as well as investments of your time. Keep your bets small so that failure, which is likely, doesn't hurt you too much.

Recognize Risk-Reward Asymmetries

In a world of exponential growth, if you bet too small relative to the theoretical optimal amount, you're making a very small mistake. You still make a lot of money if things go well and you get on the right side of exponential growth; you just don't make quite as much money as you would have if you had bet more. And by betting "too small," you have a lower chance of going broke.

By contrast, betting too big relative to the optimal amount brings the catastrophic outcome of going broke into play. And when you're broke, you can no longer benefit financially from long-term exponential growth. Betting too big relative to the optimal amount gets you very little in a world of exponential growth. Your overly large investments mean you make more in the event things go well, but you were already going to make a lot. In the event things don't go well, overly large bets can easily bust you.

Avoid All "Can't-Win" Situations and Time Traps

The concept of avoiding all "can't-win" opportunities is as simple as it sounds, but I think it takes most people decades to learn. If the best that can happen to you from doing a thing is not very good, and the worst thing that can happen to you is very bad, then you shouldn't do that thing.

This is a concept with broad application. If you lend money to someone you met recently, the best that can happen is that they pay you back, and the worst that can happen is that they don't pay you back and you spend a lot of time and energy worrying about it. Very asymmetric. If you follow your friends down a double black ski slope, and you are not a double black skier, the best that can happen is you get down the mountain uninjured and have a story, and the worst that can happen is that you sustain a major injury that alters your lifelong health trajectory.

Activity Should Add Value . . . Otherwise, Rest and Contemplate

This is not a good time for dilettantism; your midlevel efforts are not value-enhancing. When it comes to investments of your time and money, it's a very bad time, historically, to do things halfway.

What technology has done is create one global playing field, where the expected standard for everything is excellence. In a previous generation, the question was sometimes posed: "Would you rather be a big fish in a small pond, or a small fish in a big pond?" Being a big fish in a small pond used to be a highly sustainable and lucrative possibility. Technology and globalization have now mostly eliminated this strategic option.

My advice for young people is: Avoid spreading your tentacles too far; pick one thing to specialize in and do it well; only branch out if you demonstrate sustained success and have a strong urge to try something new; and when you are not engaging in the one thing you do well, you should relax, because our connected world, while thrilling, is also demanding and exhausting. Remember that sitting out has strategic value—you get to learn without cost or risk.

In a highly competitive global world, you might reasonably expect to have a small edge on your competition when it comes to your specialty. However, it is also reasonable to expect that you are at a large negative disadvantage if you venture into new fields. A poker player might expect to earn one big blind per 100 hands in the game he specializes in, but lose ten big blinds per 100 hands in a game that's relatively new for him. This is the danger of dilettantism; it might take you ten hours doing the thing you're good at to overcome the losses from one hour spent doing the thing you're bad at.

Think of sports gambling. Suppose you've been watching soccer your whole life and are an astute soccer handicapper who can bet profitably against sports books. The information embedded in market prices is so good that, if you are right about your abilities, your best expectation after paying juice is to make a small profit of perhaps 1 percent on every dollar bet. But if you are wrong about your abilities, and in fact have only average knowledge (this is likely the case), you are lighting your money on fire, losing perhaps 4–5 percent of every dollar bet.

Gratuitous Risk without Edge Can Be Ruinous

At a poker table once, someone I respect said, "Everyone I know who's ever bet on props has gone broke at some point." I puzzled over this, because a prop bet, in poker terminology, is a bet on something where the odds are fair, such that there is no expected edge for either player. An example would be if players bet even odds on whether the flop would have more black cards or red cards. I realized that, strangely, my friend's observation was probably right; betting on props is a potentially catastrophic decision, even though the expected financial loss is zero.

The reason for this is subtle and is beyond the scope of this book. There is a class of mathematical models called Risk of Ruin that examines the probability of going broke as a function of starting bankroll, betting edge, bet sizing, and number of bets. A good introduction to these models is provided in Bill Chen and Jerrod Ankenman's book *The Mathematics of Poker*.

Play around with these models for a while and you'll come to several quick conclusions. The first is that the probability of going broke at some point is quite high even if you do have a positive edge and a decent-sized bankroll. I'm always surprised at how high the probability of ruin is for various starting assumptions I plug in. The second lesson is that, if you spend from your bankroll (withdrawing winnings for spending rather than bankroll padding), the probability of going broke at some point increases massively. The third lesson is that the probability of going broke is strongly a function of betting edge: If you even occasionally engage in zero-edge or negative-edge betting, the risk of ruin increases astronomically. Needless to say, the way most poker players do things—engaging in some low- or no-edge betting while spending heavily from their bankroll—almost guarantees ruin.

Place a Subjective Value on Your Time

Money and time are closely related—you can usually spend money to save time. I believe that such trades should generally be made wherever possible. The way I suggest handling this is to have a subjective value for your time that reasonably reflects your life situation. For a long time, my subjective value of time was $100/hour, and my subjective value of administration time was $150/hour. If I could save an hour of time, I'd pay $100 to do it, and if I could save an hour of painful time, like doing paperwork or paying bills, I'd pay $150 for it.

The real trick in all this is to save time without adding complexity. For example, at various times, I've had a personal assistant. It is a no-brainer: If you can, hire someone at $25 an hour to do things like grocery shopping, cleaning, and errands, and save your time and energy for higher-value projects. However, adding a personal assistant has its own costs above the $25 an hour that you pay them; you lose privacy, you have to communicate exactly what you want, and they might make costly mistakes.

The Rule That Worked for Your Parents and Grandparents Probably Won't Work for You

The financial rule that worked well for your grandparents' was: Buy assets, and, whatever you do, never panic and sell them. If your grandparents followed this rule, and had income that exceeded expenditure, chances are they did fairly well. It was nice to be long assets of any type during the postwar era in the United States, perhaps the greatest bull market in assets the world has ever known. Depending on their age, your parents might have dealt with a slightly trickier environment, as both the dot-com crash and the financial crisis of 2007–09 brought severe challenges. That said, if they started accumulating assets in the 80s, and simply held, they did well.

It's not clear that this strategy will work well for future generations. There's a nontrivial possibility that the world will come apart at the seams. This might not happen. But there's a distinct possibility that it could happen, and a good personal life strategy will allow for it. A full analysis of the challenges is beyond the scope of this discussion; I encourage those interested in the details to check out my previous book, *Setting Sun: The End of US Economic Dominance*. A short list of the problems, from long horizon to short horizon, runs like this: climate change, nuclear proliferation, wealth and income inequality, wave of Baby Boomer retirement (started in 2008, peaks in 2025) with associated entitlement spending on Social Security and Medicare, $1.4 trillion student debt load, growth of the Federal Reserve from $800 billion to $4.5 trillion, government control of the housing market, monetization of the federal debt and associated corruption out of Washington, DC. This is a US-centric list, but the rest of the developed world is facing very similar problems. If you look at all periods of history, in all places, and note the lack of stability, and then consider the present and note the obvious and extreme imbalances, it's reasonable to conclude that instability is extremely likely going forward.

4 TIME

Managing your time requires courage. The day-to-day time management decisions you make are irreversible. Time, once spent, is gone forever, in all but memory. Your mind and body proceed, but move toward dissolution. As adults, we plot our way through time, knowing that our physical and mental capabilities are in steady, inexorable decline. The trade-offs we make in managing time are therefore vastly consequential.

Your desire for stimulation will ensure that complexity always follows you. No matter how diligent you are in seeking to minimize complexity, it will always be there. But you must continue to try to simplify whenever possible.

Managing your time well comes down to not being overwhelmed by friction. The degenerate is more prone to energy variability than the non-degenerate and has to be particularly vigilant against overreach and complexity. The degenerate has a tendency to expand endeavors in high-energy periods, only to be forced to contract them in low-energy periods. This wastes time, because you need to organize your activities once (when you increase them) and then again after the costly pruning.

Even though you're a degenerate, your approach to time management should be somewhat cohesive and well thought out. Do you utterly hate all forms of physical exercise? If so, your personal strategy must involve eating somewhat less than your exercise-loving counterparts, and you should try to fit in low-grade exercise like casual walking whenever possible. Do you loathe administrative detail? If so, your optimal time-management strategy should be to minimize personal administration. But you should strive to spend much less money than your work-loving counterparts, and you should also take on fewer projects and responsibilities.

In managing your time, it is critically important to know your preferences. Your preferences determine your optimal allocations of time. For example, if you don't like work, a good personal organization strategy for you involves spending less time at work. If you don't love spending time with people, your equilibrium involves being less social. If you don't like managing people, try not to be a manager.

Around 2009, things were going quite poorly for me, and my good friend Kenny Tran analyzed my downtrend in this way: "You're like an octopus—you spread your tentacles too far when things are going well."

As I've aged, I've realized that maintaining a level of simplicity in one's affairs is the single most important element of time management and organization. As a degenerate, you're not likely to be good at bringing simplicity to your life, but you should always strive for it.

Degenerates are degenerates because they are in some ways excitable. They enjoy stimulation and expansion into new domains. The majority of artists in all places and at all times in history have been of degenerate temperament. Degenerates, who are more prone to variations in energy than most, tend to want to focus their high-energy periods on the expansion of activities.

The expansion of your domain is inherently more stimulating than the contraction of it. The problem is that your high-energy, high-capability self (the version of you that is most prone to the execution of activities) is often incompatible with your low-energy, low-capability self. And unfortunately, it's often the low-energy, low-capability version of you that is left to manage, maintain, and repair whatever complicated apparatus or plan the high-energy you has created.

The solution for the degenerate is not to cut off the expansion of activities that comes in high-energy periods. The solution is to be cognizant of the ongoing management costs associated with taking on additional levels of complexity. Also, since we are most capable, organizationally, in high-energy periods, it's always best to contract existing commitments in high-energy times. A substantial fraction of high-value time, when you have energy, focus, and motivation in abundance, should be spent in contracting your activities. Conscious contraction is a worthy investment of high-energy, high-capability time.

When possible, do things in such a way that they stay done, and avoid situations where this is impossible. At all times, new activities should be carefully considered and added only when value far exceeds cost. Be especially careful about adding activities that entail an ongoing, almost never-ending commitment of time and energy. Anytime you add these things, the maintenance complexity of everything goes way up. This can apply to: social media, paid work, investment, a partnership or joint/group project, club duties, or any social understanding (a regular monthly dinner, etc.).

An error asymmetry can result when you take on (or don't take on) additional complexity. If you choose not to take on additional complexity, you will tend to: a) do a better job on your existing projects and commitments, and b) have time and energy free if unexpected and especially compelling opportunities present themselves. You will also tend to be more relaxed. If you do choose to take on new complexity, you will tend to: a) do a slightly worse job on your existing projects and commitments, and b) be impatient, and not have the time and energy to appreciate especially compelling opportunities when they come up.

In a hypercompetitive world, the things you do poorly will hurt you much more than the things you do well can ever help you. Suppose, for example, that you undertake to trade your own stock portfolio. If you do a very good job managing your portfolio, your best-case scenario is to do about as well as the overall market, after accounting for risk differences; you might do better or worse, but mostly due to chance. However, there are about a hundred things you could do to perform way worse than the market—you could trade way too much and incur transaction costs, you could buy into penny stocks or pump-and-dump schemes, you could take on too much risk or develop a taste for margin or options. Basically, in the market, if you do everything perfectly, your only reward is that you don't fuck things up too badly, but if you do things poorly, you will light your money on fire. This basic pattern is true in most business settings. Since it's really, really hard to find one thing you can do well (something that makes money for you), when you find that thing, you should focus most of your energy on doing it as best you can. The error asymmetry in taking on additional complexity is that, as you take on new projects beyond the one or two things you can do well, there is a risk that you do nothing well, and the consequences of this could be catastrophic.

It's important not to spend too much time communicating, or following social norms, unless you have a great need for these things. I spent most of my twenties in an environment that could be characterized as the epicenter of networking, Harvard Business School. I was one of the first few hundred people on Facebook (my undergrad students convinced me to join in the first few days of its existence), and I was a very early adopter of LinkedIn. At Harvard, I always sensed that there was an uneasy mix of "old" and "new" social rules. The old social rules applied—you were to attend weddings and birthday celebrations and be generally aware of significant life events. But the new social rules also applied—it was expected that, with the aid of the latest technologies, you would be friends with a huge number of people, including Harvard section-mates, old students, and your entire pre-Harvard network.

Something, as they say, has to give. What gives is the old social rules. People move toward small weddings, no birthday celebration, sporadic gift-giving, and quick/thoughtless communication. On the whole, though, all of this occurs slowly; the individual strives to live by the old social rules and is loath to give them up. The new social rules and old social rules coexist uneasily, and the result is extreme busyness.

Your philosophy of personal organization is really your all-encompassing strategy for how to approach life. Michael Porter has said that "the essence of strategy is that you must set limits on what you're trying to accomplish." My personal philosophy on organization is that I don't want to spend all my time communicating. (You might be different.)

As we adjust to new technology, I believe it will be necessary to come to view incoming communication as an offer for interaction rather than as a to-do list item. Ignoring is the path to simplicity for the message receiver, and the most effective way for society to deal collectively with a surfeit of messages of all types. It's very important that your investment of time and energy be generated by your own desire for outputs, broadly construed. You should spend your time and energy to accomplish and experience what you want to accomplish and experience. Don't allow other people's inputs (messages of various kinds) to be the determinant of how you spend your time and energy.

There is a real opportunity cost to an overinvestment in social life—mainly, figuring out stuff on your own. Many people would be better off spending more time reasoning things out for themselves, and far less time listening to others' opinions. There's a real sense in which time spent socializing crowds out time that could be spent thinking. And, just as taking on new projects is fun, and contracting projects when necessary is not fun, meeting new people is a lot of fun, and contracting social life is not fun.

As technology has become more important in our lives, it's crucial for all of us to have a strategy for dealing with it. It is possible to achieve technological leverage, where you are using technology to save time and amplify your achievements. It's also possible for technology to eat up your time, your attention span, and your money. Striking a balance is not easy.

My personal view is to overspend a bit to stay on the technological frontier in most things. I'd characterize my strategy as "cutting-edge with scheduled replacement": I tend to buy the best available option or close to it, and then replace it at a roughly planned interval of two to three years. This is a matter of personal taste, however, and I could imagine that a strategy of keeping old technology for a long time might also be good. The crucial thing to remember is that new technology and new apps that come along are an option for you, not a necessity. The best approach is probably minimalist: Stick with a few apps and technologies that have a proven ability to amplify your energy and time, and avoid taking on new complexity whenever possible.

My approach to technology—stick to a few proven winners and spend up for the best—also applies to hiring professionals. One of the best pieces of business advice I've ever heard is, "Have a Rolodex of people, all of whom actually do what they say they will do." This is, by the way, about 5 percent of people. If you do cultivate the list and get down to the people who truly do what they say they are going to do, and do it well, you should be willing to pay dearly to hang on to those people. The increase in your capabilities—your ability to leverage your own time—will more than justify the expense.

I think that, when hiring professionals to complete tasks for you or to otherwise save you time, it's reasonable to have a subjective value of your own time, and then hire people either when: a) you can't do what they do, or b) the cost of hiring them, including the costs of organizing and communicating with them, is less than the subjective value of your own time.

As a degenerate, some of the things you absolutely hate are: rules, process, discipline, and routine. However, the value of all these things goes up in highly complex environments. And the world and your career environment are extraordinarily complex. Find a few personal organizational processes that work for you, and try to stick with them. As a degenerate, you need to be tight, organizationally, a small fraction of the time, so that you can be loose the majority of the time.

The particular rules, processes, disciplines, and routines you take on will be a matter of personal taste. Mine are a bit peculiar. I keep most of the details I need to track in life in two places—in notebooks, and in a few different spreadsheets. I try to update these carefully at least every other week. I don't really store stuff—I just make sure my notebooks and spreadsheets are correct when I'm using them, and throw out most of them after a reasonable time.

You will probably want some rules in place for dealing with communication. One simple piece of organizational advice to keep in mind is this: If you are overly busy in general, strive to increase cycle times. Respond to non-urgent conversations more slowly. Cycle times cannot speed up indefinitely, but we sometimes act as if they should. Keep expectations about your response times low; make cycle times longer.

In the future, I expect an explosion of information, messages, and communication channels. At the same time, expectations for a quick reply will get higher. Simply ignoring more messages than before is probably the answer in personal settings. But in professional settings, you will continue to be expected to reply faster and faster. I am typically against life prescriptions for other people, but if I have a hope for the society of the future, it would be: Don't feel guilty about being somewhat slow in your communication. Communication is not a to-do list item. It's an offer for interaction. Ignoring is the path to simplicity. This is simply where society has to go in the presence of ever-increasing communication technologies. The fact that we sometimes seem to be going in the opposite direction—with more and more communication technologies AND increasing expectations for quick responses—is simply terrifying.

5 COMPETITIVE EDGE AND CAREER PLANNING

Developing a career strategy in a world defined by technology and global competition is an extreme challenge. Today's "knowledge workers" now have to ask the question: Am I providing incremental value over Google? Rapid technological advancement is making that a higher and higher bar.

On the plus side, we live in a world with exponential growth around every bend. Learning to do just one value-added activity can be exceptionally wealth-enhancing in a world with technology and a global community of more than 3 billion Internet users.

A theme of this chapter is that technology and a global marketplace open up possibilities for individuals to harness exponential growth in their careers like never before. An important part of career strategy today is putting yourself on the right side of exponential growth.

The beauty of exponential growth is that it presents asymmetric risk-reward. A person who invested in Facebook at its IPO (or, better yet, started working there in the early days) had limited downside but unlimited upside. Whenever possible, strive to put yourself in these spots, where the gains to be had are far bigger than the potential losses.

You should seldom, if ever, engage in activities where the benefits are slight and the potential losses are large or catastrophic. An example in the world of finance might be investing in 30-year Treasury bonds (where the yield is only 3 percent but the potential capital losses, if yields rise, are huge). In everyday life, driving fast, riding a motorcycle, and even skiing are examples of activities that yield only slight benefits, whereas the downside can be significant.

There are two terms from gambling that are useful in evaluating asymmetries: positive freeroll and negative freeroll. A positive freeroll is a situation in which nothing bad can happen, but something good can happen. In a negative freeroll, nothing good can happen, but something bad or very bad might happen. In a gambling context, making a bet with someone who can't or won't pay you is an example of being negative-freerolled. An example in finance might be a lawyer buying shares in a company that he knows is about to be subject to a takeover bid; if his information is somehow wrong, the stock declines and he loses money. If the stock goes up, there is a high probability that he will be caught for insider trading and be forced to forfeit a multiple of his gains (or worse).

In your career, there are ways to harness the power of exponentials—for example, through marketing. If you don't place a high value on the time spent doing it, marketing can represent something like a positive freeroll: You end up with an audience that values your content, and—again—audience growth is exponential. It is very hard to go from an audience of 50 to one of 100; but it's very easy to go from an audience of 2,000 to an audience of 2,050. Although it seems like everyone is into "marketing" and "personal branding" in some way, most people with valuable content should try it, because of the risk-reward asymmetries.

The business strategy called "real options" is applicable to personal career strategy, arguably more so now than in any previous era. The crux of it is this: Sometimes, by not pursuing a particular path, you are shutting off all related paths in the future. But pursuing some costly path might open up valuable unseen future opportunities. Given a narrow short- to medium-term decision context, you should take opportunities that seem marginal or even slightly negative, because valuable unforeseen options might open up in the future. Consider, for example, Facebook's decision to purchase Oculus, and to aggressively pursue the business of virtual reality. Facebook is in the business of social networking, not VR. In the short to medium term, an investment in VR might seem distracting and low- to negative-return; the investments seem value-destroying in a narrow, short-term context. But if Facebook chooses to ignore VR while other companies with an interest in social networking, like Google, pursue it, they might never be able to catch up to Google in the event that VR becomes important to social networking. Moreover, if it turns out that, in the far future, VR is a more valuable space in tech than either social networking or search, then Facebook would have forfeited all the opportunities associated with VR as a result of an early decision to ignore it. A decision to invest in VR opens up a huge number of future options, many of which might be unforeseeable at present, while a decision not to invest risks closing off all of these options.

When students ask me which majors to pursue, my advice is usually: Err on the side of doing the hard things early. There is a steep decline in attention span for difficult study that comes with age, as well as some decrease in raw mental processing power, so it is wise to concentrate your most demanding studies in the early years. You could conceivably learn computer science or advanced statistical techniques in your thirties, but it's unlikely. A major in, say, computer science opens up many future options and shuts off very few.

Herbert Simon wrote that "a wealth of information creates a poverty of attention and a need to allocate that attention efficiently among the overabundance of information sources that might consume it.[1] Since what is scarce is always what is valued, the ability to focus attention will be an increasingly difficult skill to maintain, and will also be what is valued by the market. It will not be a fun process for anyone, but attention span management will be crucial to your overall career strategy. Whenever you find yourself manically checking scores, or browsing social media photos, or engaging in five electronic conversations at once, remember that these activities are probably taxing your attention span, and harming your long-term ability to focus.

---

[1] H. A. Simon, "Designing Organizations for an Information-Rich World," in *Computers, Communication, and the Public Interest*, ed. Martin Greenberger (Baltimore, MD: Johns Hopkins University Press, 1971), 40–41.

Attention span management in today's world probably means: having your attention span decline slower than everyone else. Everyone is becoming somewhat manic and unfocused. We can debate why this is true, but a reasonable hypothesis is that one's ability to focus is more easily harmed than helped, and so, over time, even those trying to protect their attention span will see it degrade as technology makes everything faster. Remember that scattered, distracted behavior will rarely get you paid; it is the ability to focus when others can't that has value.

Another piece of advice I give to students and recent graduates: Keep expenses low, because you increase your options by doing so. Those whose expenses are systematically high have fewer potential options than those whose expenses are low. When your expenses are low, you can move, study, or pursue new opportunities with much less friction than you can when expenses are high. The same advice applies to romantic partners, pets, possessions, and real estate ownership; recognize that the benefit of having them comes at this cost of higher friction in pursuing new paths. Such commitments also make it harder to correct mistakes when your trajectory veers off course.

The opening paragraph of this chapter suggested that you design your career to develop "incremental value over Google." Technology and globalization have made almost every field more competitive than ever before. We can expect that increased levels of specialization and competition will be the norm in every field. Being a jack-of-all-trades and a master of none isn't a good strategic path.

6 TILT, OR SENSITIVE DEPENDENCE ON INITIAL CONDITIONS

In poker, the word "tilt" is used to describe a state of irritation that affects one's play adversely. Severe tilt happens in poker, but anyone prone to it can't last long in the game. Poker players more commonly suffer from low-level, garden-variety tilt, a minor irritation that, at the margin, impels them to make slightly suboptimal decisions about when to bet, call, raise, or fold.

Poker players, in their strange vernacular, refer not only to tilt involving suboptimal decisions at the table but also to "life tilt," which happens when irritation and uncertainty cause them to make sustained irrational and unwise decisions in their life away from the tables. Needless to say, sometimes poker tilt fuels life tilt.

I think that there are two primary sources of tilt: regret and obviously bad choices. In poker and in life, if you attempt to operate on too little sleep, or on a substance of some sort, or while arguing with someone via text message, you're unlikely to make good choices in a sustained way. This chapter will focus on regret tilt, which results from wishing things in the recent past had gone differently.

In my experience, poker tilt and life tilt stem from a common source: We're aware that life is acutely path-dependent, and when things go poorly, we dwell on the fact that, had some prior event gone differently, we might have avoided our current predicament. Tilt is therefore very closely related to regret and to counterfactual thinking, the idea that had some event not happened, everything after would have been much better. Regret and the tilt it inspires are deeply anti-rational. The rational being maximizes his future welfare based on his current endowment.

Poker players, despite being highly rational, are also analytical and reflective. They are prone to counterfactual thinking and regret. Convincing yourself that regret is anti-rational will not eliminate or reduce the experience of regret. I won't waste more space here on the irrationality of regret, because regardless of how forcefully I make that case, you will still experience it.

I'll focus instead on practices that, in my experience, reduce the incidence of regret or its negative effects. Let me start with what doesn't work. Focusing on the positive tends not to work. Thinking back to times when a series of events went your way on a sustained basis seems like it should work, but it doesn't. As I've said, convincing yourself that regret is irrational likewise does not work. And what really, really does not work is any kind of "I just need to get back to even" action. By this I mean an extreme action that is self-justified on the grounds that, should it work, you will no longer be in a state of regret.

In dealing with tilt, in poker or in life, an option is: Do nothing. So much of success is just failing slower than other people. There's no better way to fail quickly than to tilt, and so, when you're tilting, you should try your best to quit all activity. If you're playing in a poker game, quit. If it's a tournament, fold. If you manage a hedge fund, go have a long lunch, drink some wine, and take a nap. When you're on tilt, just quit making consequential decisions. You cannot make good decisions in a fast-moving present when you're stuck in the past; when you're on tilt, minimize the number and complexity of any decisions you need to make.

Journaling is a practice that is helpful for some people in managing tilt. I used to keep a journal and I found it very valuable, but I no longer do, simply because I don't find the actual task of journaling enjoyable (no matter how short the entries). It's time-consuming and encourages a backward-looking mode of thought. Its value as a tilt-reducer, however, is this: When you're in a tilted emotional state, the tendency is to think that things have been bad for an extended period; but if you consult your journal, you will usually find that the "extended run" of bad times in fact started very recently. Journaling can give you a sense of perspective and balance over time. Reviewing a journal in good times serves little purpose, but in bad times it can be invaluable.

Keep an "in-session journal" by recording key poker hands that occur over time; this can help reduce tilt, in my experience. Why does it work? What happens during poker tilt is that you become stuck in the past. New hands are being dealt, but your mind is still reviewing previous hands—you're looking for where mistakes might or might not have been made. You're completely irritated by a backlog of previous hands that were unsatisfactory. Irritation, rather than rational thinking, starts to govern your play. During extreme tilt, the irritation is so severe that you are willing to gamble in the simple hope of changing your negative mental state. This, of course, hardly ever works out. It's why I advise you to err in the direction of doing nothing, in poker and in life, when you're in the tilt state.

Revert to a core of stable, value-enhancing activities. The deeper the tilt, the more certain you should be that any new activity is value-enhancing. Life tilt is often accompanied by a genuine uncertainty about whether you are making, in an overall sense, good decisions.

In the short term, you are in a negative emotional state. Things are going against you, causing you to make bad decisions. In addition to things going poorly in the short term, you are confused about the way your environment has changed, and this makes you uncertain about whether you are making good long-term decisions. Part of recovering from tilt is sitting back and untangling which of your bad results are caused by short-term factors and which are caused by long-term factors.

In poker, the skill hierarchy is constantly shifting. There is no guarantee that the best player one year will still be the best player a couple of years hence. Over the long term, many of the dominant players who are unseated by newer, more skillful players show a high tendency to not understand that the environment has changed. They continue to play the new, better players until they go broke or near broke. The difference between those who go broke and those who don't, in my experience, is the ability to recognize a changing environment. I view this as closely related to the concept of tilt recovery, for reasons I will discuss below.

In terms of concrete advice, there are four things you can do when you're on tilt to make sure you get back on stable footing. The key in all cases is to leave a very uncertain environment, where things are not going your way, and move to a simpler environment, where you are sure that what you are doing is value-enhancing.

So, first, gravitate toward dedicated learning. This is harder than it sounds, because when you're on tilt, your attention span tends to go toward zero. In poker, I think a major reason that the young are always unseating the old is that the old gradually lose their appetite for learning, and their skills ossify. At no point is learning more difficult than during the tilt state, but dedicated learning is a good place to spend your time, because it's a clear value-enhancing activity.

Second, gravitate toward easy games, broadly construed. In poker, this would mean dropping down in stakes and playing against lesser opponents, where you are sure to be a favorite. In business, it might mean cutting down on extraneous activities and focusing on a few simple things (or even one thing) that is known to be profitable. It's important to focus on easy games when you're on tilt, because there is an error asymmetry in activity selection. In an easy game, the upside is that you will make a little money; the downside is minimal. In a tough game, the upside is high, but the downside is potentially catastrophic.

Third, get a coach. On tilt, you are often too emotionally entrenched to take an objective view, so it can be useful to hire someone whose skills and viewpoint you respect to give you an objective opinion on where you stand. A good coach can give you a meta analysis of how your place in the larger scheme of things might have changed. He can help you understand how your poor results might be attributable to: 1) poor short-term decision making, 2) bad luck, and 3) a possible change in the environment such that people have passed you by, and your skills relative to them aren't what you think they are.

Fourth, create structure: Try to develop some type of schedule and routine. Tilt is generated by psychic chaos that ensues when things go poorly in an environment that you don't fully understand. A simple schedule and routine will allow you time to understand the ways your environment has changed, and will let you think about new ways to fit in. Importantly, a routine and schedule allow you to make these assessments at a time when your emotions are in the process of calming. You need to remove yourself from turbulent environments when you're on tilt—otherwise, you risk a vicious cycle of worse and worse decisions. At some point, you have to regroup, assess the damage, and move forward.

ABOUT THE AUTHOR

Brandon Adams taught undergrad economics courses at Harvard for nine years in game theory, behavioral finance, and international macroeconomics. He's a regular in the biggest poker cash games and tournaments, and has appeared on Poker After Dark, High Stakes Poker, and multiple televised final tables. He was the lead research assistant for Michael Lewis' The Big Short, and he has self-published several books. He enjoys fantasy sports, and has a website dedicated to daily fantasy sports analytics (www.advancedsportsanalytics.com).

Made in the USA
San Bernardino, CA
30 March 2019